Out
of the
Maze

PUTNAM

Out
of the
Maze

An A-Mazing Way to
Get Unstuck

Spencer
Johnson, M.D.

PORTFOLIO / PENGUIN
PUTNAM

Portfolio/Penguin
G.P. Putnam's Sons
An imprint of Penguin Random House LLC
375 Hudson Street
New York, New York 10014

Most Portfolio books are available at a discount when purchased in quantity for sales
promotions or corporate use. Special editions, which include personalized covers, excerpts, and
corporate imprints, can be created when purchased in large quantities. For more information,
please call (212) 572–2232 or e-mail specialmarkets@penguinrandomhouse.com. Your local
bookstore can also assist with discounted bulk purchases using the Penguin Random House
corporate Business-to-Business program. For assistance in locating a participating retailer,
e-mail B2B@penguinrandomhouse.com.

ISBN 9780525537298 (hardcover)
ISBN 9780525537304 (ebook)

Printed in the United States of America
1 3 5 7 9 10 8 6 4 2

"I can't believe that!" said Alice.

"Can't you?" the Queen said in a pitying tone.
"Try again: draw a long breath, and shut your eyes."

Alice laughed. "There's no use trying," she said:
"one can't believe impossible things."

"I daresay you haven't had much practice,"
said the Queen. "When I was your age, I always did it
for half-an-hour a day. Why, sometimes I've believed
as many as six impossible things before breakfast."

—LEWIS CARROLL

Imagination is more important than knowledge.
Knowledge is limited. Imagination encircles the world.

—ALBERT EINSTEIN

Contents

The Story Behind
OUT OF THE MAZE

The story of *Who Moved My Cheese?* was originally created by Dr. Spencer Johnson to help him deal with a difficult time in his life. After years of sharing his little fable with others and seeing how much it helped them in their lives and work, he made the story into a short book.

Within six months of publication, Spencer's little parable had more than one million hardcover copies in print, and within five years, more than 21 million copies. In 2005 Amazon reported that *Who Moved My Cheese?* was their number-one best-selling single book title of all time.

Over the years Spencer's beloved classic has found its way into homes, companies, schools, churches, the military, and sports teams. It has spread around the world in many foreign languages. Its readers and fans have reported that the wisdom they found in reading the story has improved their careers, businesses, health, and marriages. Its appeal has been universal.

Yet Spencer felt there were still some unanswered questions.

"Many people who read the original story," he wrote in his notes for this sequel, "wanted to know more about *why* and *how*. Why do we adapt sometimes and do well in changing times, while at other times we don't? And how can we adapt in a changing world sooner and more easily, so we're happier and more successful, however we define what 'success' is for us?"

The answer to those questions, Spencer felt, could best be found and expressed by taking the *Cheese* story one crucial step further.

Who Moved My Cheese? showed its readers a pathway for adapting to change in their lives and work.

Now *Out of the Maze* provides the tools to help you step onto that path and not only adapt to change, but change your destiny.

Foreword
by Emerson Johnson, Austin Johnson,
and Christian Johnson

We are very happy that you are about to read *Out of the Maze*.

From an early age, our father always enjoyed looking for ways to help people. When he was a teenager he started a swim school to help other neighborhood kids swim. As a young adult he trained as a surgeon, then discovered his true passion was writing. Through his writing he felt he could be of service to a greater number of people.

We miss him dearly and are incredibly proud of his contributions to the world.

He himself often used the words and aphorisms in this story, throughout both the highs and lows of his life. When he was diagnosed with pancreatic cancer, they helped him view his illness in a new light before he passed. They gave him the tools to embrace the change he was facing with love and gratitude.

At the end of the story we have shared a letter he wrote in the final stages of his illness, which we feel illustrates the extent to which he used these insights within his own life.

We hope you enjoy this book, and wish you the very best.

The Johnson Family
July 2018

A Seminar
Chicago

ONE CRISP AUTUMN day, a group of people met for another session of a weekly business development seminar. This was their next to last class, and for today they had been assigned to read a little story about two characters, Hem and Haw, who each responded very differently to change. The book was called *Who Moved My Cheese?*

Dennis, the seminar leader, called the class to order.

"Okay, everyone, I want to start off with a question: Who the heck *did* move our cheese, and what are we gonna do about it?"

The students laughed. Dennis had a way of putting them at ease, yet they also knew he had some serious insights when it came to business.

They began discussing the book. Some said they had gotten a lot out of the story, both in their work and in their personal lives.

Some, though, had questions.

"I get the whole thing about adapting to change," said Alex, who worked in the tech industry. "But that's easier said than done. How exactly do we go about *doing* that?"

Mia, a doctor, agreed. "Some changes seem easy to go with. But some seem really difficult."

"And my job hasn't just changed," Alex added. "Seems like it's disappearing completely."

"Me, too," said Brooke, who was in publishing. "Sometimes it feels like I don't even recognize the field I'm in anymore."

"Sometimes I don't recognize my *life* anymore," said Alex. The others laughed. "Seriously," he said. "So much is changing at once. I'd '*Move with the cheese*' if I could—but half the time I have no idea where the cheese even went!"

While this was going on, a young man in the back, Tim, raised a hand and said something.

Dennis put up both hands to stop the action, and once everyone else had quieted down, he asked Tim to repeat his question so they could all hear it.

Tim cleared his throat and said, "What about Hem?"

Alex turned to look back at the young man. "What *about* him?"

Tim said, "Whatever happened to him?"

The room fell silent, as everyone thought back to the story of Hem and Haw and asked themselves the same question.

"That's what I want to know," Tim continued. "Because honestly, Hem is the character in the story that I most relate to.

"Haw seems to catch on and find his way. Meanwhile Hem is sitting back there in his empty house, alone and upset. Seems to me, he wants to figure this all out just as much as Haw, but he's genuinely stuck. And I hate to say it, but that's pretty much how things are for me, too."

At first, nobody said anything. Then Mia spoke up.

"I know what you mean. That's kind of how my situation feels, too. I *want* to go where the cheese is. But I don't even know where to begin."

One by one, they realized how much they resonated with what the young man said. In the story, the Haw character went out and found "New Cheese." He went with the change, and it worked out for him. But Hem was still lost.

A lot of them felt that way themselves.

All that week, Dennis thought about the young man and his question.

When the class gathered the following week, he said, "I thought a good deal about your questions from last week, about why Haw changed but Hem didn't, and what might have come next.

"I think there's more to the story, and I'd like to share it with you."

The place got so quiet you could hear a mouse blink. Everyone wanted to know: *What happened to Hem?*

"You probably remember the events of *Who Moved My Cheese*," Dennis began . . .

The Original Story of
Who Moved My Cheese?

ONCE, LONG AGO in a land far away, there lived four little characters who ran through a maze looking for cheese to nourish them and make them happy. Two were mice named Sniff and Scurry, and two were Littlepeople named Hem and Haw.

The Maze was a labyrinth of corridors and chambers, some containing delicious cheese. But there were also dark corners and blind alleys leading nowhere.

One day they all found their favorite cheese at the end of a corridor in Cheese Station C. After that, they kept returning to the same place every day to enjoy more of that wonderful Cheese.

It wasn't long before Hem and Haw had built their whole lives around Cheese Station C. They had no idea where the Cheese came from, or who put it there. They just assumed it would always be there.

And then one day, it wasn't.

When they saw that the Cheese was gone, Sniff and Scurry set off right away in search of New Cheese.

But not Hem and Haw. The two Littlepeople stood there, stunned. Their Cheese was gone! How was this possible? No one had warned them! It wasn't right! This was not the way things were supposed to be.

They spent days being upset.

Finally Haw noticed that Sniff and Scurry had run off into the Maze, and he decided to follow the mice and go look for New Cheese, too.

"Sometimes, Hem, things change and they are never the same again," said Haw. "This looks like one of those times. Life moves on. And so should we."

And so saying, he left.

After a few days, Haw showed up again at Cheese Station C with a few small pieces of New Cheese, and offered some to Hem.

But Hem didn't think he would like this New Cheese. It wasn't what he was used to. He wanted his *own* Cheese back. So Haw reluctantly set off again on his own to look for more New Cheese.

And that was the last Hem had seen of his friend Haw.

The *New* Story:
What Happened Next . . .

FOR DAYS, HEM stayed in his home by Cheese Station C, pacing back and forth, fussing and fuming.

He still expected more Cheese to appear every day, and couldn't believe it when that didn't happen. He felt sure that if he stood his ground and waited it out, things would turn around.

But they didn't.

And why didn't Haw come back? Hem came up with many different answers as he paced.

At first he told himself, "He *is* coming back. He'll be here any day now, and things will go back to normal." But it had been "any day now" for days, and Haw still wasn't here.

As he grew still more upset, Hem's thoughts took a different direction.

"He forgot about me."

"He's hiding from me."

"He's doing this on purpose! How could my friend betray me like this?"

This last thought made Hem angry, and the more he focused on it, the angrier he got.

He was angry that Haw had left him alone, angry that the Cheese was gone, and angry that nothing he did seemed to fix or improve the situation. Finally he stopped and shouted, "IT'S NOT FAIR!"

Worn out from pacing and being upset, Hem collapsed into his favorite armchair and began to brood.

What if Haw got lost?

What if he'd been hurt, or worse?

Hem forgot about being angry and just thought about his friend, and about what terrible things might have happened to him.

After a while a different question occurred to him. Instead of "Why hasn't Haw come back?" he began to wonder, "Why didn't I go with him?"

If he had gone with Haw, he reasoned, maybe things would have been different. Maybe Haw wouldn't have gotten lost. Maybe nothing bad would have happened to him. Maybe they would be eating Cheese together right now.

Why didn't he *move with the Cheese* like his friend did?

Why *didn't* he go with Haw?

The question gnawed at him, like a mouse gnawing on a piece of Cheese.

Meanwhile, he was getting hungrier and hungrier.

Hem got up out of his chair again to do some more pacing, and he tripped over something on the floor. He bent down and picked it up. It was only after he blew off the dust that he recognized it.

It was an old chisel.

He remembered the day when he held that chisel while Haw whacked at it with a hammer until they made a big hole in the wall of Cheese Station C, looking for new Cheese. He could almost hear the sound of the hammer and chisel echoing off the walls of the room.

Ping! Ping! Ping!

He poked around on the floor until he found the hammer they had used, and blew the dust off that, too. He hadn't realized till that moment just how long it had been since the two of them, Hem and Haw, had gone looking for Cheese together.

He missed his friend. And he was starting to worry. All this time he still expected more Cheese to appear, and for Haw to come back.

But there was still no Cheese, and no Haw.

He had to *do* something. He could no longer stay home and wait. He had to go out into the Maze and search for Cheese.

Hem rummaged around, found his running shoes, and put them on, the way he and Haw used to do when they were first exploring for Cheese. As he began to lace them up, he reviewed what he knew about the facts of the situation.

He knew that he had to find more Cheese. If he didn't, he would die.

He knew that the Maze was a dangerous place, full of dark corners and blind alleys that led nowhere. So he had to be very careful.

Finally, he knew that if he was going to get through this, find more Cheese, and survive, it was up to him. He was on his own.

He wrote all this down on a piece of paper and put it in his pocket, so he wouldn't forget.

The Facts of the Matter

1) I have to find more cheese.
   If I don't, I'll die.

2) The Maze is a dangerous place,
   full of dark corners and blind
   alleys.

3) It's up to me. I'm on my own.

Knowing the facts of the matter felt reassuring to Hem. At least he knew where things stood.

He looked at the hammer and chisel. Maybe they would help him in his journey ahead, exploring the deeper recesses of the Maze.

He picked up the tools, put them in a bag, and slung it over his shoulder.

Armed with The Facts of the Matter, and a strong hammer and chisel, Hem ventured out into the Maze.

FOR THE NEXT few days, Hem wandered through corridors, working his way deeper and deeper into the Maze. The corridors were empty, except for a few small rocks here and there. No sign of Cheese.

Every time he came to a new chamber, he poked his head inside to scan for Cheese. But every single chamber was empty.

Every so often, he would come to a dark corner. When that happened, he would quickly turn back and head the other way. He was determined not to get lost.

Now and then, he passed by a blind alley. He would peer down, just to make sure, and when he saw that it ended in nothing but a brick wall and darkness, he would hurry on his way.

Here and there, Hem could see that Haw had passed by that way, because Haw had scratched notes on the corridor walls, each note framed with a drawing of Cheese. They made no sense to Hem.

Anyway, he was too hungry and too tired to stop and read.

There was still no sign of any Cheese at all.

As he explored, Hem kept thinking about that question that had gnawed at him, turning it over in his mind again.

Why didn't he go with Haw?

To be honest, Hem had always thought of himself as the brains of the pair. Haw was a fine Littleperson and a good companion, with a cheery disposition and a good sense of humor. More of a copilot than pilot, though. That's what Hem always thought.

Now he wasn't so sure.

"Why *didn't* I go with Haw when I had the chance?" he murmured to himself.

Was it because he was stubborn? Or just plain foolish?

Or, was he just a bad Littleperson?

Hem thought about that as he walked through corridor after corridor. "Maybe this is punishment for something I did," he said out loud.

The worse he felt about himself, the more his energy dropped, though he did not notice this. He was not even aware of the thoughts he was having about himself as they ran through his mind, like little mice in a maze.

Then he had a thought so terrible it froze him in his tracks. "Maybe it's my destiny to run in circles in the Maze forever."

Hem felt his legs about to give out. He leaned against the corridor wall and slid to the ground.

On the opposite wall was one of Haw's notes:

Old Beliefs
Do Not Lead You
To New Cheese.

Hem just shook his head.

"Oh, Haw," he murmured. "What were you thinking? Cheese is either there or it's not. *Beliefs* have nothing to do with it!"

For the first time, he wondered if Haw might have gotten too weak to go on and simply given up. He wondered if that's what was happening to himself right now.

All at once he felt alone and afraid.

Nothing was the way it used to be. Before, the Maze was where Hem and Haw had worked and had a social life. They both grew up there and built their lives there. The Maze was Hem's world.

But the Maze had changed.

Now, it seemed as if *everything* was different. Haw was gone, Sniff and Scurry were gone, the Cheese was gone, and he was out wandering the corridors, getting weaker and weaker. Hem didn't understand why all this was happening.

The Maze had become a dark and scary place.

He curled up on the floor and fell into a troubled sleep.

HEM STIRRED AND felt his foot bump up against something on the floor where he lay. A few somethings. He sat up and looked at them. They were round little rocks, about the size of one of his fists.

He picked one up and felt its smooth, shiny red surface. It wasn't a rock at all. It smelled good.

In fact it smelled so good, Hem wanted to take a bite.

He shook himself. What was he thinking? Whatever this was, it certainly wasn't Cheese.

It might be dangerous.

He looked around and almost jumped.

There was another Littleperson sitting nearby, watching him! It wasn't Haw, and not any of their old friends, either. Hem had never seen this Littleperson before.

He didn't know whether to smile and say hello, or to be afraid.

The Littleperson lifted up one of the little red not-rocks and held it out toward Hem. "You looked hungry," she said.

"But I can't eat this," said Hem. "It isn't Cheese!"

"Isn't what?"

"Cheese," Hem repeated. "It isn't Cheese."

She didn't say anything, just looked bemused.

"Cheese is another word for 'food,'" Hem explained patiently. "Everyone eats Cheese. Even the mice."

"Ah," said the other Littleperson. They were both quiet for a moment. Then she said, "*I* don't. I've never even seen 'cheese.'"

Hem found this hard to believe. A Littleperson who didn't eat Cheese? Impossible!

The Stranger was still holding the little rock out toward Hem. He looked at it and shook his head.

"Whatever it is, I can't eat it," he said. "I only eat Cheese."

He lay back down again, feeling hopeless. After a few moments, he half-heard the Stranger say:

"I'll bet you can do a lot more than you think you can . . ."

But Hem had already drifted off again.

When Hem opened his eyes a few hours later, he felt hungrier than he'd ever felt in his life. It's dinnertime! he thought. And then the reality of his situation came rushing back.

No Cheese. No dinner.

He sat up. The Stranger was gone, but the little red rocks were still there. He picked one up and smelled it again. It smelled sweet.

Before he had time to think about what he was doing, he took a bite.

It was crispy, but also juicy! Sweet . . . but tart! It tasted like no Cheese he had ever eaten. He ate the whole thing. He couldn't help it.

He lay back and groaned. "What have I done?" he said. "I ate a rock!" He was sure he was going to die.

He drifted off to sleep once again.

And for the first time in days, he slept all through the night.

When he awoke the next morning, the Stranger was there again, sitting on her haunches with her arms wrapped around her knees, watching him.

"You're not dead," she said.

"No," said Hem. "I'm not, am I."

In fact, he felt a little stronger.

The Stranger was holding out another rock to him. Hem took it and ate it. It certainly wasn't Cheese, but it was tasty, and as he ate he felt his energy returning, ever so slightly.

The Stranger talked to him while he ate his rock. Her name was Hope, and she lived nearby, at a place called Fruit Station A. "Fruit," she said, was what the rocks were called. She also said they were called "apples."

By this time, Hem was on his third Apple.

Hope told Hem that the fruit had been getting scarce lately, and that for the past few days she had been exploring different parts of the Maze, looking for new supplies.

"It used to be that every day when I woke up, there would be more apples," she said. "But that's been happening less and less.

"Actually," she said, pointing to the piece of fruit Hem was now eating, "that's my last one."

Hem stopped mid-bite and looked at her. "You mean, they're *gone*?"

She nodded. "They just stopped showing up. I don't know why."

Hem looked at his mostly eaten Apple, then at Hope again. "You gave me your last Apple?"

Hope shrugged. "You looked hungry."

"I was," said Hem. "But aren't you hungry, too?"

"A little," she admitted.

Hem thought about all the Apples she had given him to eat, and realized he'd never thanked her.

"Thank you," he said.

"You're welcome," she said.

Hem shook his head, amazed. "Eating these things actually made me feel better," he said. "I can't believe it!"

Hope smiled and said, "Sure you can. It's not hard, if you just let go and try."

This confused Hem. Just let go and try what? He had no idea what she was talking about.

He knew one thing, though: He was still hungry.

All this talk about eating reminded Hem why he was out here in the Maze in the first place. Now that his strength was starting to return from eating the strange new food, it was time to go looking for Cheese again.

So far he had failed in his quest—and he knew exactly why that was.

"I just haven't tried hard enough," he explained. "What I need to do," he said, "is go explore the parts of the Maze I haven't tried yet."

Hope shrugged. "I'll go, too. If that's okay with you."

(Hope didn't yet see just how they were going to get out of their jam, but she had no doubt at all that they would.)

Hem nodded grudgingly. It couldn't hurt to have some company. As he got to his feet, he noticed again that curious note that his friend Haw had scratched on the wall:

Old Beliefs
Do Not Lead You
To New Cheese.

"Maybe not," he said to the note on the wall. "But I'll tell you what *does* lead to New Cheese: Trying harder!"

So saying, Hem slung his bag of tools over his shoulder and the two set off, trundling down corridor after corridor, poking their heads into chamber after chamber, and carefully avoiding the dark corners and blind alleys.

Every chamber they found was empty, but Hem had resolved not to give up.

As they walked, Hem told Hope about the old days. About how he and Haw and their friends Sniff and Scurry would go looking for Cheese every day, and how it used to be abundant and easy to find. There for the taking. All they had to do was look up and down a few nearby corridors, and there it would be.

"Simpler times," he said. And he fell silent as they walked on.

Times had changed. Hem was not the same Littleperson he used to be. He once was strong and proud, someone other Littlepeople looked up to because he was so sure of himself.

But the disappearance of the Cheese had changed all that. Events had taken their toll. He was no longer strong, and no longer so proud.

As he reflected on all this, it occurred to Hem that he felt less sure of himself than he used to. He could see that his usual confidence had been shaken.

This was something new for Hem.

He had never really noticed his own thoughts before, or taken a step back to consider how he looked at things.

To him, how he saw things was just the way things were.

As they walked the corridors, the two found a few crumbs of Cheese here and there, enough to nibble on and slow the gnawing in Hem's stomach.

Hope tried a few bits of cheese, too, and she liked it just fine.

Every now and then they found an Apple, just sitting on the ground by the wall, which they split between them.

Between the nibbles of Cheese and the occasional Apple, it was just enough to get them back to their starting point, where they would rest up for the next day's search.

Every day when they set out, Hem felt he had less energy than the day before.

When they returned to the same spot again after hours of fruitless search, Hem would drop his bag of tools and slump down against the corridor wall, feeling even more exhausted.

One day as they returned, Hem felt so discouraged he didn't know if he could keep going much longer. All he could think about was how heavy his tool bag was.

"That must weigh a lot," said Hope.

"It's not that bad," said Hem. He didn't want to admit how much it weighed or how drained he felt.

"Why do you bring it with you every day?" she asked.

"It's for us to make holes in the wall," said Hem. He explained that if they found the right wall, he would ask Hope to hold the chisel, the way he used to do, and he would swing the hammer, the way Haw used to do.

"Ah," said Hope. Then she said, "Has that worked for you before?"

"Of course it has," said Hem, though what he was thinking was, She asks *a lot* of questions. "This is the finest chisel money can buy!"

"What I mean is," said Hope, "does making holes in the wall actually find you more cheese?"

Hem didn't answer. He felt offended. These were good tools! He put down the heavy bag with a loud *clunk!* and sat back against the wall.

Hem missed Haw. He didn't like being way out here in the Maze, so far from home. He wanted things to go back to the way they were.

"You miss your friend," said Hope.

It was a little unnerving, how she always seemed to know what he was thinking.

Hem shrugged. "I just wish things would go back to the way they were."

Hope sat down next to him and leaned back against the wall, too.

"I know," she said. She glanced over at Hem. "But I'm not sure that's how it works."

"What do you mean?" snapped Hem. He was getting a little annoyed.

"I don't think things *ever* go back to how they were," said Hope. "Here's my thought, though: Maybe they can turn out *better* than they were."

Hem didn't see how.

"Our *trying harder* plan isn't working out, is it," said Hope softly.

Hem didn't answer. He felt too miserable.

"Maybe we need a different strategy?" she added.

Hem glanced over and saw that she was looking up at Haw's sign, the one that said, *"Old Beliefs Do Not Lead You to New Cheese."*

"What if we tried a new belief?" said Hope.

Hem shook his head. "You don't *try* a belief. Your beliefs are just . . . there!"

Hope glanced back over at Haw and cocked her head. "But what if you decided to change one?"

"That's not how it works," Hem explained. "Besides, I like my beliefs just the way they are! If I changed them, who would I be? I wouldn't be Hem!"

He did not want to change or let go of his beliefs, because he thought they were what made him who he was.

"Bet you'll change your mind," she murmured.

"Why would I do that?" Now Hem was getting irritated. "I like my mind just the way it is!"

Hope shrugged again. "I like it, too. But we still haven't found any cheese."

Hem didn't have an answer for that.

They were both silent for a minute. Finally Hope got to her feet and said, "Well, good night, Hem. Sweet dreams. I'll see you in the morning."

Hem sat against the wall, frowning. He was thinking about what Hope had said about his hammer and chisel.

Of course putting holes in the wall wouldn't do them any good. Hadn't he already known that? So why *was* he lugging around these old tools?

Because he didn't know what else to do, that's why.

They would never find Cheese. He would never find his friend Haw. He would die here in this corridor, with his useless bag of tools.

Hem let out a very big, very long sigh, and then he asked himself the question that had nagged at him ever since his quest began:

Why didn't I go with Haw?

And with that, Hem began to cry.

Before long, he fell asleep.

THAT NIGHT HEM had a dream.

In his dream, he saw himself back in his home by Cheese Station C, pacing and fussing and fretting and fuming. Something was different. But what?

Then he saw what it was. There were bars on the windows! It looked like he was in a prison. Looking in at himself through the bars, he saw how unhappy he was. In his sleep, he cried a little more.

He woke up in the middle of the night, thinking about the dream. It baffled him. Why was he like that, a prisoner in his own house, missing his friend yet refusing to go with him?

Hem lay awake on his back for hours, thinking about this. He thought about it until dawn came.

In the early light, he could just make out Haw's scratched note on the wall, about old beliefs and New Cheese.

"Maybe Haw was right," he said quietly. (Thinking out loud helped him to make his thoughts clearer, especially the more difficult thoughts, like the ones he was having now.)

He thought about the day Haw left, so long ago now. Haw had tried to talk to Hem about what he thought they needed to do, and Hem had refused to listen.

"I was sure I was right, and Haw was wrong," he said. "But maybe I wasn't right. I didn't trust Haw, but I did trust my own thoughts."

All at once, Hem sat up straight.

Old beliefs. That's what Haw's note was about. But Hem had never stopped to think about what a "belief" *was*.

Now he thought he knew.

He clambered to his feet, picked up a sharp stone, and wrote his own new thought on the wall, next to Haw's. When he was finished, he drew a picture of one of Hope's Apples around it, so he would remember that it was his note and not Haw's.

A Belief
Is A Thought
That I Trust
Is True.

That's all a belief was. A thought. But look at how much power it held!

Why didn't he go with Haw to look for New Cheese? Because Haw was looking at things differently—and Hem couldn't see what Haw saw. His own thoughts had kept him there in Cheese Station C, because he trusted that they were true.

He had believed that if he stayed and stood his ground, things would turn around.

He had believed that Haw was going off on a fool's errand, and that he, Hem, knew better.

His beliefs were keeping him trapped in his way of seeing things. *That* was why he didn't go with Haw.

Suddenly he understood his dream. The bars on his windows were his old thoughts, thoughts he trusted were true, but which actually prevented him from venturing out into the Maze.

His beliefs were holding him prisoner!

He scratched out another new note on the wall, and surrounded this one, too, with a drawing of an Apple.

An Old Belief
Can Hold You
Prisoner.

He pictured himself pacing back at home in Cheese Station C, and how he kept thinking that if he just waited, the Cheese would start appearing again, and things would go back to the way they were.

That was another thought he trusted, wasn't it. Another belief that held him prisoner!

So, did *all* beliefs do that?

He thought back to the day he woke up and first saw Hope, and how she had held out an Apple for him to eat. At first he was afraid to eat it, but then he ate it anyway. He had trusted her. And she gave him her last Apple! She was a good friend to him.

Hem thought *that* was a belief that served him well.

He wrote another note on the wall:

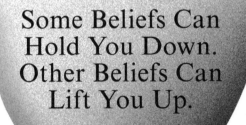

Some Beliefs Can
Hold You Down.
Other Beliefs Can
Lift You Up.

He thought back to Hope saying, "What if we tried a new belief?"

What had he replied? "You don't *try* a belief. That's not how it works!"

Maybe Hope was right, though. Maybe you *could* change an old belief, and choose a new one.

He tried to think of an old belief right now, but he couldn't come up with one. This whole "belief" business was still a new way of thinking for Hem, and he wasn't sure how it all worked.

He looked up at the notes he had just made, with the drawing of the Apple around each one. He remembered the first time Hope had tried to offer him a piece of fruit, and how he'd said, "Whatever it is, I can't eat it. I only eat Cheese."

That was what he'd thought, and he'd trusted that thought—but it turned out it wasn't true at all! Because he ate the Apple and felt better. So Cheese *wasn't* the only kind of food he could eat.

And now he thought differently.

What did Hope say? "I bet you'll change your mind." And she was right. He had!

He wrote quickly on the wall again:

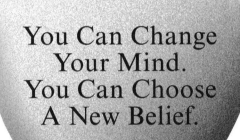

You Can Change
Your Mind.
You Can Choose
A New Belief.

Hem noticed that he felt totally energized, and this surprised him.

In the past, Hem did not like it when someone challenged his beliefs. He resisted changing his mind, and felt offended when anyone suggested that what he was thinking or saying might not be true.

But now, instead of feeling bad that he'd been wrong, he felt excited by what he was discovering.

He realized that, before, he had resisted changing his mind because he felt threatened. He had not wanted to change his beliefs, because he *liked* his beliefs. He had thought they made him who he was.

But now he saw that wasn't so. He could choose a different thought. He could choose a different belief.

And he was still Hem!

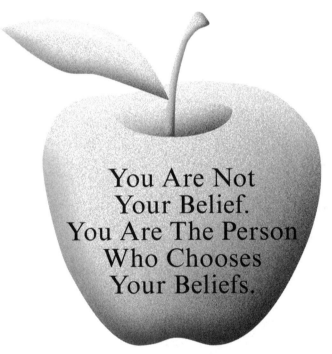

You Are Not
Your Belief.
You Are The Person
Who Chooses
Your Beliefs.

"So here's the real question," he said, pacing back and forth as he thought out loud. "Now that I know what a belief is, and how much power it holds, and how easily I can choose a *new* belief . . . what should I *do*?"

He stopped pacing.

The answer was obvious. He should use this new knowledge to help him finish their mission. He should go find more Cheese and Apples.

The problem was, they'd already tried everything. There wasn't anywhere else to look. There weren't any more Apples or Cheese to be found. They were out of options.

It was an impossible quest. And if that was the case, then there wasn't really any point in trying.

But . . . what if the "impossible" part was just another belief? Could he change it?

He felt a tingle run up his spine.

What Would You Do
If You Believed
It Was Possible?

"Hang on, though," Hem told himself. "Let's be reasonable."

This belief business could go only so far. After all, there were limits here. Right?

Hem held that thought for just a moment. Then he took a breath, let go—and felt it begin to change!

He looked at the sharp stone in his hand, and wrote once more on his wall of notes:

There Are
No Limits
To What You
Can Believe!

WHEN HOPE SHOWED up a few hours after dawn, she found Hem sitting up, polishing his running shoes, and humming to himself.

She hardly recognized this new Hem! When she left him the evening before, he was tired, defeated, and grumpy. Now he looked more refreshed than she'd ever seen him.

She looked at the series of new notes on the wall, each one surrounded by the outline of an apple.

"My, my," she said. "You've been a busy Littleperson."

Hem nodded. "Yup."

"What happened?" she said.

He looked up at her. "I changed my mind," he said.

"Good," she said. She looked at all his notes again, then back at him. "About what?"

Hem put his shoes down and got slowly to his feet. (He was still stiff and sore from dragging around that heavy bag of tools.)

"I haven't figured that part out yet," he said.

Hem knew that what he'd been doing before wasn't working. He needed to do something completely different. And that meant he needed to look at things completely differently. He needed to change his mind and choose a new belief.

But what belief, exactly? He didn't know.

Hope came over and sat down next to him again.

"Mind if I ask you something?" she said. (She could see Hem was deep in thought and probably didn't want her to disturb his concentration, but this was something he needed to hear.) "You said your cheese just stopped showing up? Like my apples?"

"That's right," said Hem.

"Here's what I'm wondering: Before, when your cheese was still appearing fresh every day—where did it come from?"

Hem started feeling annoyed again. Hope asked so many questions! And what did it matter where the Cheese came from? It was gone now.

He stopped.

Hem looked over at Hope and thought about the question she had just posed.

Where *did* the Cheese come from?

Had he ever asked that question before? Had Haw? He thought back, sorting through all the memories of times they had spent together, looking for Cheese, finding Cheese, and enjoying Cheese. Had they ever, even once, asked themselves this question?

They hadn't! He was sure of it.

Hem felt his pulse quicken. He didn't know why, but this felt important.

He looked at Hope again, all traces of irritation gone now. "Where . . . did the Cheese . . . come from?" he repeated slowly. "You know, I think that might be a *very* good question."

Hope's eyes sparkled. "Does that mean you've got the answer?"

"Well, no," said Hem. "But it still seems like a good question. If we keep asking it, maybe we'll find a good answer!"

They were both quiet for a moment.

Then Hope looked over at Hem and said:

"I wonder what's outside the Maze."

Hem stared at her. "What's outside the *Maze?*" He shook his head in disbelief. "There's *nothing* outside the Maze."

What a thought! Outside the Maze? That made no sense at all. The Maze was all there was. There wasn't any "outside."

"Ah," said Hope. She paused, then looked again at Hem and said, "Are you sure?"

"Of course I'm sure!" said Hem.

They looked at each other, and then they both burst out with the same words at the same time:

"A thought you trust is true!"

Another belief! And it seemed to Hem that this might be the kind that held him down, rather than lifting him up.

Could he change his mind about this one, too?

Hem shut his eyes and tried to imagine a place outside the Maze. In his imagination, though, all he could see was the Maze itself, just as he had always known it.

He opened his eyes again and shook his head. "It's no good. I'm not seeing it." He looked at Hope. "All I can see is what's *in* the Maze. I can't picture anything outside it."

The Maze, after all, was all Hem knew. He had been hemmed in all his life.

Hope looked at him thoughtfully. Then she said, "What if you just believe it first? Maybe *then* you'll see it."

"That's—" *That's crazy!* was what Hem was about to say. Instead, he said, "That's . . . a great idea."

If there really were no limits to what he could believe, then why not give it a try? He closed his eyes again and began to think:

There is something amazing outside the Maze.

Hem took a big breath and felt the new thought fill up his mind, and as he did, he felt himself trusting it.

He opened his eyes and wrote another note:

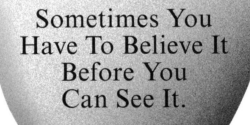

Sometimes You
Have To Believe It
Before You
Can See It.

He looked at Hope and said: "*Let's go find out what's outside the Maze.*"

She smiled. "Sounds good to me. Maybe we'll learn where your cheese comes from."

He nodded, excited at this thought. "And your Apples, too!"

Hope got to her feet. "I'm in," she said. "How are we going to do it?"

"I have no idea," said Hem.

And he truly didn't. Where would they look? He couldn't imagine. They'd already looked *everywhere*.

Hem remembered when he and Haw used to go looking for Cheese. They always avoided the dark corners and blind alleys. He explained this to Hope, then waited to see if she would come up with another good question.

And of course, she did.

She said, "What if those dark corners are not all dark?"

"How can they not be dark?" said Hem. "After all, that's why they're called *dark* corners!"

Hope reached up and took down a thick candle from a sconce on the wall. "Not if we bring a candle."

Hem was already up and starting down the corridor when he noticed Hope hadn't moved. She was looking down at his sack of tools.

"Are you bringing your hammer and chisel?"

Hem looked down at the tools, then slowly shook his head. "I don't think so."

"Good," said Hope. She smiled. "I don't think it works to launch a new quest with old baggage."

They went back into the corridors they had already explored many times, only now they went looking for dark corners instead of steering clear of them. It felt strange to Hem, seeking out the very thing he had always avoided, but he decided that feeling strange was probably part of the process.

Soon they came to an impossibly dark corner, and stopped.

They turned into the darkness, and Hope lifted her candle to light up the little passageway.

Hem's heart sank. The candle's light shone just far enough to reveal that the passageway ended in nothing but darkness and a flat brick wall.

"Another blind alley," he said.

Hope looked thoughtful. "That's what I'm thinking, too," she said. "But what if that is not a thought we should trust? After all," she added, "not all dark corners are dark. Maybe not all blind alleys are blind."

Hem liked that thought. He decided to see if he could hold on to it and trust it enough that it would turn into a belief.

He closed his eyes and tried once more to use his imagination. For several long moments, nothing happened . . . until, just as he was about to give up, he caught a glimpse of something flickering at the edge of his thoughts—as if he were seeing, if not a light, at least the *possibility* of a light. He felt his heart give a leap.

Hem opened his eyes again and looked at Hope.

"Let's try it," he said.

The two walked slowly into the passageway, both feeling nervous as they walked. Hem couldn't help thinking, The Maze is a dangerous place. He had known this all his life, ever since he was a young boy. *The Maze is a dangerous place . . .* The thought kept whispering in his mind.

But what if *that* was not a thought he should trust was true?

He stopped walking, and Hope stopped, too, waiting to see what he would say.

"Just because you think it," he murmured to himself, "doesn't mean you have to believe it."

You Don't
Have To Believe
Everything
You Think.

Hope didn't say anything. She understood what was going through his mind.

They continued walking. Sure enough, as they got closer Hem saw there *was* a tiny light at the very end of the alley. It was the candle itself, reflected in a small window set into a door!

They opened the door and stepped inside a small chamber, much like the many chambers they had already explored. In the dim light of Hope's candle, they looked all around the bleak little room. Four corners. Four walls. Nothing else.

It was completely empty.

Disappointed, Hem turned to go, but Hope stood still, watching him, as if waiting for him to say something.

"What," he said. "It's empty."

"Looks that way," she said, and she waited some more.

So Hem thought about it—and then he asked himself a question:

If not all dark corners were dark, and not all blind alleys were blind, then could it possibly be that not all empty chambers were empty?

"On second thought," he said, "shall we take a second look?"

Hope smiled and took his hand. "Let's!" she said.

They walked along the first blank wall, turned the corner and walked the second blank wall, turned another corner, walked halfway along the third wall—and stopped.

"Do you feel that?" whispered Hem.

"I feel it," Hope whispered back.

Cool air wafted across their legs. Hem bent down and sniffed at it. It smelled incredibly fresh.

They got down on their hands and knees, and down at knee level they found an opening in the wall, just big enough for a Littleperson to pass through.

Hem glanced over at Hope and gestured with one arm. *After you.*

Hope crawled into the tunnel. Hem followed.

With Hope leading the way, they crawled and crawled, until they both began to see a light at the end of the tunnel.

The light grew brighter and brighter . . . and then all at once—

HOPE AND HEM emerged into a brilliant light, so dazzling that at first they couldn't see a thing. They stood upright, blinking, and inhaled the clean, fresh air.

As their eyes got used to the light, they looked around. They were standing in a beautiful green meadow, with a cool, gentle breeze blowing.

Hem had never seen or felt anything like it before. He looked up at the ceiling, if that's what you could call it. It was so blue, and so high up! And there was a dazzling golden light up there, brighter and warmer than any light he had ever known, too intense to look at directly.

Hem was speechless. He took a deep breath, put his hands in his pockets, closed his eyes, and turned his face up to feel the warmth.

His fingertips felt something in his pocket. He pulled it out and looked at it. It was a piece of paper. At the top it said "The Facts of the Matter."

He began to read.

And then he began to laugh.

Hope smiled, puzzled. She had never seen Hem laugh before. She didn't think she'd ever seen him even smile.

"What," she said. "What does it say?"

Hem showed Hope the piece of paper.

"It says, I have to find more Cheese, and if I don't, I'll die." He looked at Hope. "But I found Apples instead, and ate those, and I didn't die."

She looked at him. "No, you didn't. I knew you wouldn't."

"It also says the Maze is a dangerous place, full of dark corners and blind alleys."

She nodded. "And it was a dark corner that led to the blind alley that brought us here."

"The last thing it says," added Hem, "is that it's all up to me. That I'm on my own."

Hope smiled. "Well, *that* one certainly isn't true, is it." She held out a little piece of cheese she had just found.

He took it and nibbled at it gratefully. "No," he said. "It's not."

As they explored the new world they were in, outside the Maze, they found Apples and Cheese everywhere.

They tried eating Apples and Cheese together. It was delicious.

And everything was so bright! They had never realized just how dim and poorly lit things were inside the Maze.

It occurred to Hem that getting out of the Maze felt just like getting out of the prison of his old beliefs.

Maybe that's all the Maze really was.

One thing was for sure: The air here smelled *so much* sweeter!

Hem looked down once more at his little piece of paper. "*The Facts of the Matter*," he said, and he laughed again. "They *seemed* like facts at the time."

Hope nodded. "But they weren't."

"No," said Hem. "Not a single one."

He turned the piece of paper over, and on the back of The Facts of the Matter he wrote down a summary of what he'd discovered over the past few days.

THE WAY OUT OF THE MAZE

Notice Your Beliefs
A Belief Is a Thought That You Trust Is True

Don't Believe Everything You Think
Sometimes "Facts" Are Just How You See Things

Let Go of What Isn't Working
You Can't Launch a New Quest with Old Baggage

Look Outside the Maze
Consider the Unlikely—Explore the Impossible

Choose a New Belief
Changing What You Think
Doesn't Change Who You Are

There Are No Limits to
What You Can Believe
You Can Do, Experience, and Enjoy a
Lot More Than You Think You Can

As they sat on the grass, enjoying the sunlight and cool breeze, Hem thought again of his friend Haw. He'd be enjoying this all even more, he thought, if Haw were with them.

"You're thinking of Haw," said Hope.

Hem nodded. As usual, she knew what he was thinking. He wondered how she did that.

"We have to go find him," she said. "And your friends Sniff and Scurry, too."

Hem looked at her, and nodded again. "That's exactly what I was thinking," he said.

"All right," said Hope. She smiled at him. "Let's go."

They both stood up, and Hope took Hem's hand once more, when suddenly—

"Hem! HEM!"

Astonished at hearing his name being called in this unfamiliar place, Hem turned and stared at the figure striding briskly toward him.

It was Haw!

"You're here!" cried Haw as he embraced Hem and thumped him on the back with both hands.

"And so are you!" said Hem. He glanced all around. "And Sniff and Scurry?"

Haw laughed. "Oh, you know them—they were the first ones out! But you, Hem . . . I was worried you'd *never* find your way out of the Maze."

"I almost didn't," admitted Hem. "I thought I was trapped in there. I thought I was going to die." He sighed. "I was wrong, but I couldn't see it. I was stuck in my old beliefs."

"So what happened?" said Haw quietly.

Hem reflected for a moment.

"First, I got angry. Then, I got hungry. Then, I found Hope." He turned to look at Hope, and smiled. "Hope, this is—"

"I'm *very* happy to meet you, Haw," said Hope as she shook Haw's hand.

"Charmed!" Haw laughed and gave a little bow, then said to Hem: "And after you found Hope?"

"Then, I changed my mind!"

Haw gave a warm smile and embraced Hem once again. "I've missed you, my friend. I'm so glad you found your way out of the Maze. And I'm even happier that you found how to change your beliefs."

"Beliefs are powerful things, aren't they?" said Hem.

The three stood silently together, contemplating the awesome ability beliefs have to hold you down, or to lift you up—and the thrilling discovery that you can change them, and still be you.

A thought occurred to Hem. "Hang on a second!" He fished in his pocket, took out an Apple he had picked up, and offered it to Haw. "Have you tried one of these?"

Haw nodded gleefully. "Apples," he said. "Love 'em."

"And they go really well with Cheese!" said the two friends in unison.

Hope cocked her head. "You know what, though?"

The two turned to look at her.

"I'll bet there are all kinds of other delicious things to eat here," she said. "Things we've never thought of before. Things we've never even imagined."

Hem and Haw looked at each other.

Was that possible?

Of course it was!

And the three set off to explore.

The End . . .
or is it another beginning?

A Discussion

WHEN DENNIS FINISHED the story, he stopped talking and looked around the room. Everyone was deep in thought. He waited.

"Wow," said Alex.

Dennis turned to him and smiled. "Wow?"

"Good for Hem," said Alex. "He did it. He made it out of the Maze."

"Just like Andy Dufresne in *The Shawshank Redemption*," said Ben. The rest of the group laughed. By now Ben had a well-established reputation as the class entertainer.

"I had a boss once who wasn't so lucky," said Brooke.

"Really," said Dennis. "What happened?"

"When I first got out of journalism school, I worked for a city newspaper. Nobody could convince the publisher we needed to get online. He believed print advertising would keep paying the bills, even when our biggest accounts switched over to advertising on the web. He insisted that paid circulation would pick up again soon, even as more and more readers left us to get their news online. A year after I arrived, the whole operation shut down."

"Never found its way out of the Maze," murmured Alex.

"Beliefs are powerful things," said Dennis. "A single stubborn belief can take down an entire company. People believe that how things have always been is how they'll always be. But it never is."

"You know what Mark Twain said," Ben commented. "It ain't what you don't know that gets you in trouble. It's what you know for sure that just ain't so."

The class laughed again.

Dennis smiled, and said, "Twain had it right, as usual, and here's an example: When the *Titanic* made its maiden voyage in 1912, people described the vessel with a single word."

"Unsinkable!" said Brooke.

"Exactly. *Unsinkable.* That's what everyone believed. And because they believed it, they didn't bother loading on enough lifeboats."

"And more than fifteen hundred people died," said Brooke.

"All because of a thought people trusted was true," added Mia.

"The *'facts of the matter,'*" murmured Alex.

The class was silent for a moment.

"Oh, man," said Ben.

"I'm starting to get the sense that *all* beliefs are bad," said Mia. "Narrow viewpoints that just get us in trouble. But that can't be true. I mean, even Hem found some beliefs that served him, right?"

"Absolutely," said Dennis. "All beliefs are worth *examining.* The key is to notice your beliefs, and test them—not necessarily *discard* them.

"Some just get in our way and stop us from being our best selves, or even drive wedges between us. But some beliefs are powerful truths, beacons that lift us up and help us keep moving forward, even in the toughest times."

"Like the idea that all people are created equal," suggested Ben. "Endowed by their Creator with the unalienable rights to life, liberty, and the pursuit of happiness."

"Or like Hem's belief that Hope was a good friend," offered Brooke.

"Or believing in our kids," added Mia.

"Or in yourself," said Dennis. "Believing in the idea that you were put here for a reason, that you have unique value to offer the world. For example: Mia, why did you become a doctor?"

"To help ease people's suffering," said Mia without hesitation.

Dennis turned to the group. "You can see that's not just a thought she thinks is true. That desire to heal? That's the *essence of Mia* showing through. Like Brooke's passion for truth and excellence in the printed word. These are core values, things that simply *are* true and never change."

"But fer cryin' out loud, everything else *does*!" put in Ben.

"Also true," said Dennis, smiling. "And that's where Hem got stuck. Circumstances change. The world turns. And things that may have been true yesterday suddenly are no longer true today.

"Blockbuster Video was *positive* we would all go on watching movies on videotape forever. Polaroid was *absolutely sure* people would always snap their photos on little paper squares. Just like bookstores in the early nineties *knew for a fact* that an online bookstore could never possibly amount to much.

"They all built their futures based on beliefs that turned out not to be true. And it sank them."

"Just like the *Titanic*," added Ben.

"Just like the *Titanic*," Dennis agreed.

He glanced around the classroom and noticed the quiet young man in the last row, frowning.

"Tim?" he said. "Anything you wanted to share?"

All eyes turned to Tim, who'd gotten the whole ball rolling the week before by asking his question, *What about Hem?*

"Yeah, I guess," said Tim. "Actually my work situation is okay. It's more a personal thing."

Dennis said quietly, "If you're comfortable."

"Sure. So, earlier this year, I found out that my parents are separating. Already *separated*, actually. Past tense."

Everyone looked back at Dennis, who said, "And that's been hard for you."

"Hard? It's *impossible.* All my life they were this constant, this bedrock. The one sure thing in my world. And they just gave up!"

"You sound angry about it," said Dennis.

"I'm *furious* about it," said Tim. "I mean, I still love them, but right now I kind of hate them, too. I just can't accept what they're doing. And what does it say about my whole childhood, is that all a lie now?"

"You know," said Dennis, "people change."

Tim shook his head. "Not like this."

Dennis considered that. "How do you think *they* see the situation?" he said.

Tim seemed startled by that thought. "I have no idea."

"What do they say?"

"They say they tried their best, and that this was the right decision for them, and that in time I'll grow to accept it. Which I totally don't believe."

Dennis paused, then said, "What if you tried . . . believing differently?"

"It doesn't work that way!" Tim blurted out. There was a silence in the room, and then he said, "Oh, wow." He looked at Dennis again. "That's exactly what Hem said, isn't it?" He gave a thin smile.

Dennis shrugged and smiled back. "Pretty much."

"So what are you saying?" said Tim. "That they made the right decision? And that it wouldn't have been *more* right for them to stick together and work things out?"

Dennis shook his head. "That's not for me to say. When looking at a belief, though, I like to use Hem's question: *Does it lift you up, or hold you down?* Does it get you out of the Maze, or keep you running in circles?"

Tim looked down at the table, thinking hard.

"Just remember this, Tim," said Dennis. "Changing what you think doesn't change who you are."

Tim looked up and met Dennis's eyes, then nodded slowly. "Yeah," he said. "Okay. I'll think about that." He paused, then added, "Maybe I'll take a crawl through Hem's tunnel, see if there's anything bright out there."

Dennis broke into a grin. "That's great, Tim." He glanced up at the wall clock. The class was just about over.

"Last week," he said, "we touched on how confusing it can be when there's so much change happening all at once. And I'm paraphrasing here, but a few of you asked the same excellent question: *Where do I start?*"

He looked around the room. "Alex?"

The others realized that Alex, who had been so vocal the week before, had been nearly silent ever since Dennis finished telling this new story.

Alex paused for a long moment, thinking hard. He began speaking, slowly at first.

"Seems to me," he said, "that it starts with *me*."

Dennis nodded, as if to say, *Go on.*

"Well," said Alex. "I've been so focused on the problems. On my changing industry, how confusing it is, how hard it is to keep up and know what to do next."

"You said you'd *move with the cheese* if you could," put in Brooke, reading from her notes, "but half the time you don't even know where it went."

"Right," said Alex. "And that's exactly what Hem was trying to do, right? Roaming all over the Maze, trying to find the solution. But where he needed to start wasn't anywhere in the Maze. It was right in his own head.

"When you said, 'Get out of the Maze,' it hit me— the maze I'm stuck in isn't my job, or my company, or even my industry. It's my own approach. The Maze I need to get out of? I think it's my own thinking."

"Maybe it's time to let go of some old beliefs," said Brooke.

"No kidding," replied Alex. "And choose some new ones!"

Ben grinned and added, "Don't forget what Hem thought about that. *There is something amazing outside the Maze!*"

The group laughed again and broke into applause. Ben stood and took a bow.

"Well put," said Dennis, with a thoughtful smile. "When you allow yourself to believe it, an entire world of new possibilities opens its doors to you. Which is quite an *amazing* thing indeed.

"And on that note, my friends, our seminar comes to a close. I want to thank you all for the great discussion and wish you the very best, in your careers and in your lives.

"And I'll leave you with this thought: If you feel you got anything of value from this little story, then I hope you will . . .

Share
It
With
Others

The following is a letter Spencer composed in the final stages of his illness, showing just how much he had embraced the principles in this book.

A Letter to My Tumor

Hello Tumor,

I love you now! I used to fear and fight you, so that I could defeat you. Then I looked at my beliefs to see if they were more about what I loved or what I feared.

Clearly they were about what I feared.

And I love how I have learned to love you, which seemed like a strange idea to me. How much richer my life has become. Because, while I am sick and realize I could die soon, I have become a much more appreciative, loving person, much closer to my family and friends, with a greater sense of purpose, and have accelerated my spirituality.

So, thank you. Thank you. Thank you!

— Spencer Johnson, M.D.

Afterword
by Ken Blanchard, Ph.D., coauthor of
The New One Minute Manager

Now that you've read *Out of the Maze,* I hope you realize the power of your beliefs and the impact they can have on your behavior and the results you get. A question you might have is, "Did Spencer Johnson only write about the power of choosing your beliefs, or did he also live by that principle himself?"

I'm happy to say that he did indeed walk his talk, but sad to give you a vivid example.

I lost my coauthor and friend to pancreatic cancer in July 2017. As you might know, when you're diagnosed with that form of cancer, it's usually bad news, as very few people survive for long. When Spencer got the word, he decided he could approach the rest of his life from a belief system based on fear or one based on love. If he chose fear, the focus would be on himself. If he chose love, the focus would be on others.

I was overjoyed with his choice to live in love. He reached out not only to close family members and friends, but also to people with whom, for various reasons, he'd lost contact, some of whom he hadn't spoken to in years.

The people I met during our visits with him were all struck by the way Spencer focused on them and their feelings rather than on his own medical condition.

During my last visit with Spencer, we were joined by Margret McBride, who had been our literary agent for *The One Minute Manager*. We called Larry Hughes, the former president of William Morrow, who had published our books, to tell him how much we appreciated his role in our lives. It was a memorable, heartwarming conversation. As I was leaving, I gave Spencer a hug and told him how proud I was of him and the positive beliefs he had chosen.

Moved by how Spencer's choice resulted in such a loving departure, Spencer's sons—Emerson, Austin, and Christian—and I were more committed than ever to making sure this book, which was so important to Spencer, got published. Even now, we can feel a big One Minute Praising coming from Spencer.

If you have enjoyed this little story as much as I have, you can carry on Spencer's legacy by sharing the book with others. I certainly intend to!

Ken Blanchard
San Diego, June 2018

Acknowledgments

What a unique contribution Dr. Spencer Johnson made to the world! One of the most beloved and influential authors of our time, Spencer shunned the spotlight, preferring to let the words of his eloquently simple fables speak for themselves. It is an honor to be able to offer *Out of the Maze* as his parting gift to the world, and we want to thank all those who made this publication possible. Our gratitude especially goes out:

To Spencer's sons, Emerson, Austin, and Christian, for their special roles in Spencer's life and for helping make this new book a part of his enduring legacy. We and Spencer's millions of readers share their loss, and are grateful for the many gifts their father left us.

To Ken Blanchard, Spencer's good friend and *One Minute Manager* coauthor; it was Ken who first encouraged Spencer to put his story down on paper so others could benefit from its simple wisdom, and who, once the book was published, became its most enthusiastic advocate.

To Hyrum W. Smith, whose long-time collaboration and invaluable contributions helped make this book possible.

To our early readers for helping this book become its best self.

To Robert Barnett, of Williams & Connolly LLP; Kathryn Newnham, of the Spencer Johnson Trust; Angela Rinaldi, of the Angela Rinaldi Literary Agency; and Nancy Casey, Spencer's executive assistant, for their invaluable support and assistance.

To Tom Dussel, Tara Gilbride, Ashley McClay, Madeline Montgomery, Chris Sergio, Merry Sun, Will Weisser, and the rest of the team at Putnam and Portfolio for their devoted dedication to the project.

To John David Mann, for his thoughtful and respectful touch in helping prepare this manuscript for publication; and to Margret McBride, of the Margret McBride Literary Agency, for her support.

To you, the reader, and to the millions of readers and fans, advocates and ambassadors of the original *Who Moved My Cheese?* story.

And finally, to Spencer himself. To call him "a master of deep truths in simple packages" would be true, yet only part of the truth. It is no accident that the future creator of best-selling fables served as both a medical doctor and a children's book author. His fondest hope was not simply to put wisdom on the page, but to give people practical tools to improve their lives, and in so doing, to help make the world a healthier, happier, and more richly fulfilling place.

Ivan Held, G.P. Putnam's Sons
Adrian Zackheim, Portfolio